The Friendship Handbook

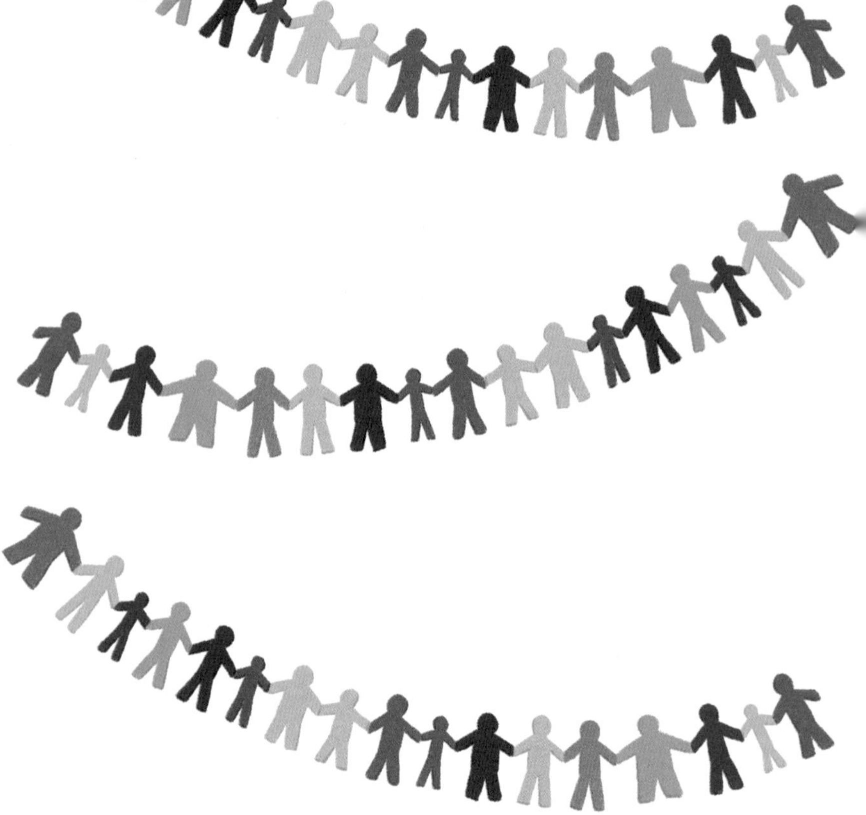

The Friendship Handbook

Poppy O'Neill

Illustrated by
Lucy Rogers

Collins

Contents

CHAPTER 1

What makes a good friend?

The most important ingredient of a good friendship is kindness. When people are kind to each other, they feel calm. This is because when you know someone's going to treat you with kindness, you don't worry so much. You can be yourself!

When someone treats you with kindness, the other ingredients of friendship can be added, like trust, respect and fun.

What does kindness look like?

- getting to know each other
- helping each other
- gentle hands
- caring about feelings
- keeping promises
- listening
- honesty

When you are kind to someone else, it makes them feel good inside. But the really amazing thing about kindness is that it makes you feel good inside too!

We are all different

Every person in the whole world is completely unique. We all have different thoughts, feelings and experiences, and personalities. When we meet someone new, it can be brilliant to find we have something in common.

What's also exciting and interesting about a new companion are the ways in which we are different.

How we look is one way we can be different or similar to our friends. Can you think of other ways? The way we draw, the jokes we laugh at, the sort of pyjamas we like to wear ... there are so many ways to be ourselves!

Most of the time, our differences make friendships interesting. Sometimes our differences mean things get tricky – like when you disagree about what game to play. When friendships get tricky, it's very important to show respect to one another.

Showing respect to others means considering the other person's feelings and accepting that their thoughts and ideas feel right for them, even if you don't agree. Respect for ourselves means telling the truth about our feelings and speaking up for ourselves. It can be difficult to respect ourselves and others at the same time, especially if we feel angry or upset.

It's not OK to hurt our friends' feelings on purpose, but we don't need to hurt our own feelings in order to take care of theirs.

We can use kind language to be honest about our feelings.

I feel furious that you drew on my picture.

I feel shocked — I was trying to be helpful. I didn't mean to hurt your feelings.

One brilliant skill for a good friendship is compromise. Compromise means meeting someone in the middle and finding a solution you both feel OK about.

What if Alex wants to play chase, but Uma wants to play catch? They can use compromise to find a solution they're both happy with.

9

When we compromise, show kindness and respect for each other's differences, we can be ourselves. Being yourself means showing your feelings, sticking up for yourself, telling the truth and sharing your ideas.

You might be thinking, 'of course I'm being myself. How could I be anyone else?' which is a very good question! Sometimes, we pretend to be like other people because we think that will make them like us more. But they would be getting to know a pretend person, not the real you.

If everybody had the same interests, feelings and ideas, the world would be a very boring place. When we let our true personalities shine, good friendships grow.

CHAPTER 2

Why do we have friends?

While it can feel good to be by ourselves sometimes, it is also nice to have someone to talk to and keep us company.

Friendships have been important to people for a very long time. The oldest existing poem, *The Epic of Gilgamesh* from about 4,000 years ago, is about a friendship between its two heroes, Gilgamesh and Enkidu.

Gilgamesh is the king of Uruk in ancient Mesopotamia, and Enkidu lives with wild animals in the forest. Even though their lives are very different, they become good friends and go on adventures together.

For hundreds of years, people told each other the story of Gilgamesh and Enkidu. Later, the poem was written down on clay tablets.

Our need to get along with other human beings is even older than *The Epic of Gilgamesh*. We need other people in order to share food and skills, and learn new things. When humans hunted and gathered their food in the wild, working together as a team meant there was more to eat and more protection from dangerous animals.

The true reason we have friends is because friends make us happy and help us when we're in trouble. When something makes us feel good and keeps us out of danger, we want to do more of it. This means that over thousands of years, human beings have developed a need for friendships.

Friends are important while you're a kid, and they'll be important your whole life too! Scientists have found that having good friends makes us healthier, happier and more resilient.

This is because having plenty of friends means we have people around us who we can relax with and who will share with us when we are in need. Knowing that we are loved and accepted makes us feel calm, and the calmer and more hopeful we feel day to day, the stronger our immune systems are. Your immune system is the way your body defends itself against illness and infections.

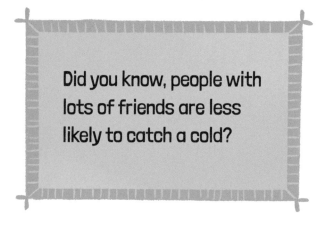

Did you know, people with lots of friends are less likely to catch a cold?

Learning how to be friends

Human beings aren't born knowing how to make friends, or how to be a good friend. It's a skill we learn by practising.

At the age of about four, children begin to understand that other people have their own thoughts and feelings that are different to their own. This means that they can begin to enjoy the ways in which they are similar and different to the other children they meet.

We practise making and being friends for our whole lives and even grown-ups are still learning.

What can I do if I don't have any friends?

It can feel very lonely when we don't have a good friend, or a group of them. Finding yourself without a friend to play with or someone to sit next to happens to everybody. It's not true that no one wants to be your friend, but it can take bravery to find a friend.

If you can find someone who seems kind or who you have something in common with, see if you feel brave enough to talk to them. You might feel embarrassed or worried, but you can also ask a trusted grown-up for help.

CHAPTER 3

Why friendships can be tricky

Having good friends is brilliant. We have fun together and can be ourselves. We feel emotions like happiness and excitement with our friends, but friendship also sometimes brings other emotions like sadness, worry and anger.

Friendship feels good most of the time, but when you feel more difficult emotions, that's not because there's something wrong with your friendship. In fact, it is quite normal, and true friends can feel upset with each other and work it out.

With a little help, we can learn to deal with the tricky parts of friendship – like being left out, feeling jealous and disagreeing. It's worth trying to work things out with our friends, because it makes friendships even stronger.

Feeling left out

One of the most difficult parts of friendships is feeling left out. It can make us experience feelings of worry, embarrassment, anger and sadness. Because friendships feel so good to our brains, when we think we've lost a friendship, it can feel very serious!

When you feel left out, you can help yourself by choosing kind, curious thoughts.

Instead of this thought:

Everybody hates me.

Try out a different one:

I can speak up for my feelings with kindness.

I wonder why they're acting differently today? I'll ask them.

23

Choosing different thoughts is a useful technique that can help us find a more hopeful and calm way to think about our friendships. A different thought might feel a bit strange at first, especially if we are used to thinking more worried or unkind thoughts about ourselves.

Think of our brains like forests, and thoughts like pathways through them. The more times we walk along a path in a forest, the easier and quicker it becomes to walk down again. In the same way, the more we think a particular thought, the easier it is to think it next time.

Nobody likes me.

I have no friends.

I can speak up for my feelings.

New thoughts take time to feel comfortable and true. With practice, their pathways will get stronger.

When friendships get tricky, it's not just our thoughts that are affected – our feelings are too. When friendships bring up difficult emotions, it's really important to take notice.

Emotions like worry and sadness can feel really uncomfortable, but it's always OK to feel them. Turn to someone you trust to talk about your feelings, and remember it's OK to cry, share a worry or ask for help.

Everybody has emotions, even if they don't show them. So, you may feel like you're the only one finding friendships difficult, but you're not alone. Sharing how we feel is one way to build strong friendships.

Bobby and Azeen have fallen out.
Bobby wanted to sit with Katie at
lunchtime and Azeen felt left out.
He's worried that Bobby doesn't
want to be his friend anymore.

It's OK for Bobby to sit with Katie, *and* it's OK
for Azeen to feel worried. Both boys have strong
feelings because they value their friendship.

I wanted to chat with Katie about a book we're both reading. I still want to be your friend — I feel angry that you think I don't.

We always sit together at lunchtime. I felt worried I'd done something wrong, and angry because I had to find someone else to sit with.

When Bobby and Azeen take the time to understand each other's feelings, they strengthen their friendship.

CHAPTER 4

Tools for being a great friend

Sometimes, you meet another person, and they feel like a friend straight away. Sometimes these connections become great friendships. But to build a lasting friendship, you need time! It takes time to get to know each other, to work out if you're a good fit for friendship and to grow trust together.

Spending time with friends, no matter how long you've known them, will make your friendships stronger.

Spending time is a bit like saving money — each time you spend time together, you're putting a penny in your friendship bank.

It's especially important to spend time with friends when one of you is going through something difficult. Perhaps you or your friend is being bullied, or a family member is unwell. Making time to be with your friends when they need someone shows how much you care.

Everyone is a "me"

Have you heard of empathy? It means imagining what it feels like to be another person. Sometimes we say "put yourself in their shoes" when we talk about empathy. But you don't need to swap shoes to try it!

When we think about what it might feel like to be another person, we can do our best to show them kindness that's just right for them.

Sam and Cleo's class are playing a game of football. Sam's team scores one goal and Cleo's team scores three goals. Sam feels disappointed, and Cleo feels proud.

The two friends feel differently about the same situation – and that's OK! They can show each other kindness by using empathy to understand each other's feelings.

Both friends can feel their own emotions and use kind language about each other at the same time – all because of empathy.

35

Speaking your mind

Did you notice how both Cleo and Sam
told the truth about their feelings? That's
another amazing technique for building
great friendships. When you speak up and tell
the truth about how you're feeling, your friends
get to know the real you.

It sometimes feels difficult or scary to say how
we feel. We may worry that our feelings might
upset others, or feel we might be wrong if our
emotions don't match our friends'. But when you
remember that everybody's emotions are unique,
it gets easier.

It's OK for you to feel how you feel, and it's OK for others to feel how they feel. It's never OK to hurt or be unkind to each other — even when someone is experiencing big feelings.

Nobody is perfect, and when you're good friends with someone, you're going to get upset with each other sometimes. The important thing is that you both take the time to understand one another, show you care and put things right.

Here are some ways you and your friends
can put things right together, when you have
a difficult time in your friendship:

- talking about what happened

- saying sorry and meaning it

- listening to the other person's point of view

- using empathy to think about how
  the situation felt for them

- showing you care about each
  other's feelings

- saying how important the friendship is
  to you.

CHAPTER 5

The science of friendship

Friendship in your brain

When we spend time with friends, our brains release three special chemicals that make us feel good: oxytocin, serotonin and dopamine. These chemicals are like a reward our brains give us when we do something that is good for our health and emotions.

When something feels really good, we want to do more of it. Researchers think that our brains reward friendliness because it helps us to guarantee a better life and keep us safe from dangers. If we need a helping hand, our friends will be there for us.

Our brains can also release these feelgood chemicals while we're by ourselves. All sorts of things make us feel brilliant!

scan of a happy brain

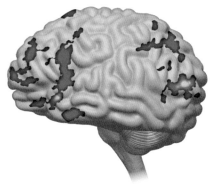

Let's take a closer look at those brain chemicals.

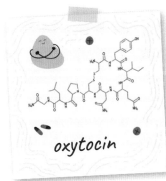

oxytocin

Oxytocin is released when we are close to others

Serotonin is released when we laugh or have fun

serotonin

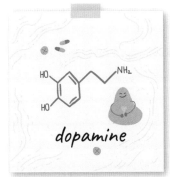

dopamine

Dopamine is released when we feel successful or understood

Circles of friendship

Friendship expert Doctor Robin Dunbar believes that human beings can have lots of different relationships at once. That's including family, friends, teachers, neighbours … everybody you know.

Doctor Dunbar says that we have lots of circles. Our parents, carers and most special friends are in the smallest, closest circle. The people we know well are next, and the people we only know a little bit are in the larger, further-away circle.

5 loved ones

You might have 15 friends you know well from your class at school and from clubs you go to. The biggest circle of friends could be the children you know at school from all the different year groups, children from your neighbourhood and the children you play with at the park. You might not know them as well so they are in the third circle.

15 close friends

50 friends

Six degrees of separation

For many years, data scientists guessed that each person is connected to every other person on Earth by just six contacts. In 2008, researchers at the computer company Microsoft discovered that it was just about true.

By studying 30 billion online messages, the researchers found that most people are just six "degrees of separation" from any other person on the planet.

Every person you know is one degree of separation from you. Your friend might know someone that you don't. You are connected through your friend. This is two degrees of separation, and so on. Isn't it amazing that we are all connected!

Below is an example of how we can connect two random people who have never met: Esme and Neelam.

Esme is friends with Jamie

Jamie's cousin is Frankie

Frankie's best friend is Charlotte

Charlotte's uncle is Simon

Simon's boss is Serena

Serena is friends with **Neelam**.

Reading fiction might make you a better friend

Did you know that reading fictional stories increases your powers of empathy? When we read about characters, we start to understand what it's like to be someone like them.

Scientists have discovered that when the hero of a book is feeling a strong emotion, our brains can experience that emotion too.

The more we practise understanding what it's like to be different people, the more our powers of empathy grow.

I'm reading a book set in a world of dragons and magic. I live in the normal world, but it still felt scary when the hero got chased by a huge dragon. I felt furious when one of the other characters stole his golden spear — it really made me loathe that character.

CHAPTER 6

Being a good friend to yourself

What does it mean to "be a good friend to yourself"? You're just one person, but there's a lot going on inside. Everybody has lots of thoughts and feelings every day that we don't have much control over. But, we can control how we respond to our thoughts and feelings.

If your friend felt sad, would you say some kind words or offer them a hug?

You can do the same for yourself. You can think kind thoughts and say kind words to yourself like "it's OK to feel sad", and giving yourself a gentle hug can bring you comfort.

The way you think and the language you use can help you work out if you're being a good friend to yourself.

When you're having a hard time, what do you think and say about yourself?

When you notice yourself thinking or speaking about yourself, ask this question:

Would I say that to a friend?

If you wouldn't say it to a friend, see if you can offer yourself a little more kindness, patience and respect.

When you listen to your emotions, it's easier to be a great friend to yourself.

CASE STUDY

Jack feels worried about going to school, because he's nervous about a test. He knows he has to go, so he pretends he's OK.

But in class, he can't concentrate. At breaktime, he can't have fun. His worried feelings are happening, even though he is trying to ignore them.

On the way home, Jack tells his mum how he's feeling. Straight away, he feels a little better. His mum gives him a hug and tells him she will talk to his teacher about ways to make the test less scary for Jack. She explains to Jack that his feelings are important and that there's no need to hide them from her.

When we feel worried, it's a message that something feels off. It could be a real danger or an imaginary one – we feel worried either way!

There are lots of ways to show kindness and friendship to ourselves when we feel worried:

Breathe deeply.
Oxygen relaxes our bodies.

Share your worry with a friend.
Talking about our feelings can make us feel less alone.

Draw a picture.
Creativity relaxes
our minds.

Have a drink of water.
Water refreshes our bodies
and minds.

Move your body.
Movement releases
chemicals that help
our mood.

Sometimes, it might feel like you need to pretend your emotions aren't happening. But this is like ignoring a friend who is trying to tell you something! Pay attention to your emotions, share them with someone you trust, and they will feel easier to deal with.

Speaking up

In friendships, there are times when we
need to speak up for ourselves. This can be
tricky if you're worried about hurting your
friend's feelings. For example, if your friend starts
to tickle you and you don't like it, it might feel
rude or unkind to say "stop".

The truth is, it's not kind to let a friend
believe that we like something when we don't.
When you say, "Stop please – I don't want to be
tickled," you're showing your friend how to be
a good friend to you. What's more, you're being
an excellent friend to yourself, as well.

Every person and every friendship is unique.
Everybody is always learning how to be a good
friend – even grown-ups.

There's no such thing as a perfect friend. If you're showing yourself and others kindness and respect, then you're doing a great job.

Finding and making friends takes time and bravery. Try your best, be yourself and you will be a great friend with wonderful friendships.

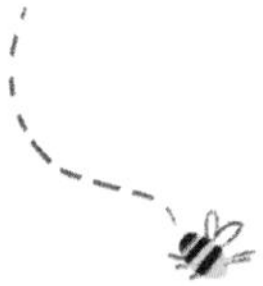

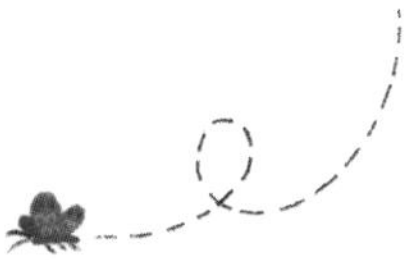

CONVERSATION STARTERS

It can be hard to know what to say when you're getting to know a new friend. One trick is to ask interesting questions, which lead to interesting conversations. Here's a list of conversation starters — pick some you like and try them out!

If you could be any animal, what would you be?

What do you like to do when it's raining?

If you could change the colour of the sky, what colour would you choose?

Do you know a good joke?

What mark would you give your day out of ten?

If you had the chance to go to space, would you take it?

If you had a treehouse, what would you keep in it?

Who is the funniest person you know?

What is the last book you read?

Which school rule do you wish you could get rid of?

If you could time travel, where and when would you travel to?

What makes someone a good friend?

CONVERSATIONS WITHOUT WORDS

British Sign Language or BSL is language that is spoken with our hands, faces and bodies. It's mainly used by people who are deaf or have hearing loss, and their hearing friends and family. Signed words can be in a different order to spoken words. Here are some BSL phrases you can use to make friends!

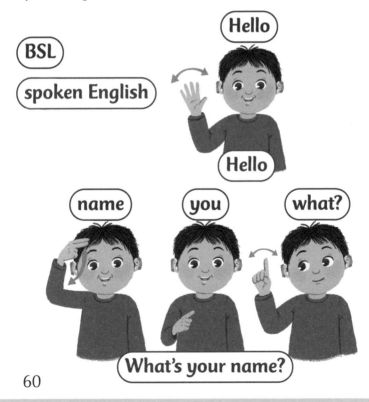

BSL

spoken English

Hello

Hello

name

you

what?

What's your name?

My name is ...

Friend

Want to play?

Do you like...?

TRY THESE GAMES WITH FRIENDS

THIS OR THAT?

Players: two or more

How to play: Take turns coming up with pairs for the other players to choose between — if you really can't decide, it's OK to say "both!". Here are some ideas to get you started:

Cats or dogs?   Swings or slides?

Cake or ice cream?   Toast or cereal?

Apples or bananas?

Why this game? This is a fun and simple way to get to know new things about people. You can play it with new friends, old friends, family members and trusted grown-ups. Perhaps you'll be surprised by the things you learn.

MIRROR BODY SHAPES

Players: two or more, in pairs

How to play: Get into pairs and stand facing your partner. Take turns to be the leader, and move your body while your partner copies you as if looking into a mirror.

Why this game? This is a very mindful game, especially for the mirroring partner. Paying attention to each other without speaking is a lovely calming activity. It can be really fun too – especially if you try not to laugh!

YOUR BRAIN LOVES MAKING FRIENDS

We don't know what other people are thinking or feeling. We have to use our own thoughts and feelings and guess what others might be thinking. This is an important skill for using empathy, and we do this every time we interact with other human beings in a friendly way.

These diagrams show how a human brain responds while the person is thinking about their own mind, a friend's mind and a stranger's mind. Scientists have found that we use a lot of the same parts of our brains to think about ourselves and our friends, and different parts of our brains to think about strangers.

**thinking about
your own mind**

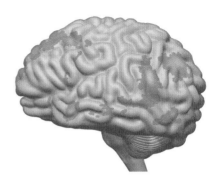

**thinking about
a friend's mind**

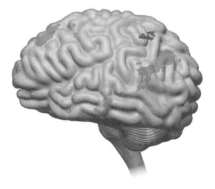

**thinking about
a stranger's mind**

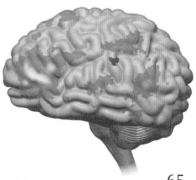

ANIMAL FRIENDS

It's not just humans who have friends – animals do too!

Dolphins recognise their friends by their unique whistle.

Chimpanzees make friends with other chimpanzees who have a similar personality.

Rooks clean their friends with their beaks.

Wild horses look out for each other and help raise each other's foals.

The longer a squirrel lives next to the same friend, the more relaxed and healthy they are.

67

SURPRISING FRIENDS

Sometimes friendship is found in the most
unusual places …

Themba the African elephant and Albert the sheep

Themba's mother died when she was six
weeks old. Albert is like a brother to her. They play
together in a wildlife reserve in South Africa.

Bea and Wilma

Bea and Wilma like to hang out together in their 65-acre safari park in the US.

Daffy and Jock

Jock the dog's owner rescued an egg from a nest that had been attacked by crows. Daffy hatched from that egg and now Jock and Daffy are good friends!

69

About the author

A bit about me …

I've been writing books for
six years, it's always been my
dream job. I live on the south
coast of England with my wife,
children and pets.

Poppy O'Neill

Why did you want to be an author?

Writing has always been my top way to be creative,
and I love reading. It feels wonderful to be able to write
the kind of books that might help readers feel good
about themselves, too.

How did you get into writing?

I studied writing at university and worked for an online
writing school called Writers' HQ. Then I contacted
a publisher to see if they were looking for new writers.
Luckily, they were and I started writing books for them,
and it's all grown from there.

What book do you remember loving reading when you were young?

I really loved the *Horrible Histories* books by Terry Deary.

What is it like for you to write?

I like to plan everything first – what's going to happen on each page or in each chapter. Then when I've finished planning, writing the words is like joining the dots. I enjoy both parts of the process, but for me they're different sorts of creativity so I prefer to do them one at a time.

Why this book?

I've had some friendships where I look back and realise that person wasn't a very good friend to me, but I didn't notice at the time. I wanted to write a book that helps readers see what makes a good friendship, so they can choose friendships that are fun and supportive.

Is there anything in this book that relates to your own experiences?

Almost all of it! I've had brilliant friendships, tricky friendships, arguments and dealt with feeling left out. We have ups and downs with our friends, but it's all worth it because friends are so important.

What do you hope readers will get out of the book?

I hope readers will learn something about themselves and their friendships – how we communicate, our emotions and how very different people can get along well together.

About the illustrator

A bit about me ...

Hi! I'm Lucy and I'm a deaf illustrator! I wear two hearing aids to help me hear. I love drawing more than anything, but when I'm not busy drawing I love to read books.

Lucy Rogers

What made you want to be an illustrator?

I've always loved poring over beautiful illustrations in children's books. As I got older I knew I wanted to work with books and due to my love of art, it was clear illustration was to be my path.

How did you get into illustration?

I studied illustration at Falmouth University which is far away down in Cornwall. There I learnt how to draw for children's books.

What did you like best about illustrating this book?

I loved coming up with all the unique characters for this book to represent the wide, diverse world we live in.

Is there anything in this book that relates to your own experiences?

Growing up being the only deaf kid in my mainstream school, I found it difficult to make friends. This book shows a lot of the things I used to do to build a new trustworthy friendship. My tip for making new friends is to ask them questions about themselves and you'll find something you both have in common!

Is it different illustrating a non-fiction book to illustrating a story?

Yes, a non-fiction book is mostly factual so must be more realistic. I love working in both non-fiction and fiction, because they are both fun and different.

How do you think pictures help the reader in books like this?

Pictures help readers to understand a little bit more about what the text is saying. They help the reader to feel more connected to what they're reading.

Would you have liked to read a book like this when you were a child?

Yes, I would have loved to read a book like this as a child, because this book's advice would have made me feel braver and more confident in making new friends. It's an important book for every kid to read.

Book chat

Which part of
the book did you
like best, and why?

Did your mood
change while you were
reading the book?
If so, how?

What did you think
was the best tip
for making friends?

If you had
to give the book
a new title, what
would you choose?

If you could ask
the author one question,
what would it be?

Did this book remind you of anything you have experienced in real life?

What was the most interesting thing you learnt from reading the book?

Is there any helpful advice for making friends that you think is missing from the book?

Book challenge:

Think of one way you could be a good friend to someone today.

Collins
BIG CAT

Published by Collins
An imprint of HarperCollins*Publishers*

The News Building
1 London Bridge Street
London SE1 9GF
UK

Macken House
39/40 Mayor Street Upper
Dublin 1
D01 C9W8
Ireland

© HarperCollins*Publishers* Limited 2023

10 9 8 7 6

ISBN 978-0-00-862463-7

British Library Cataloguing-in-Publication
Data
A catalogue record for this publication is
available from the British Library.

Download the teaching notes and
word cards to accompany this book at:
http://littlewandle.org.uk/signupfluency/

Get the latest Collins Big Cat news at
collins.co.uk/collinsbigcat

Author: Poppy O'Neill
Illustrator: Lucy Rogers
Publisher: Lizzie Catford
Product manager and
    commissioning editor: Caroline Green
Series editor: Charlotte Raby
Development editor: Catherine Baker
Project manager: Emily Hooton
Content editor: Daniela Mora Chavarría
Phonics reviewer: Rachel Russ
Copyeditor: Catherine Dakin
Proofreader: Gaynor Spry
Typesetter: 2Hoots Publishing Services Ltd
Cover designer: Sarah Finan
Production controller: Katharine Willard

Collins would like to thank the teachers and children at the
following schools who took part in the trialling of Big Cat
for Little Wandle Fluency: Burley And Woodhead Church of
England Primary School; Chesterton Primary School; Lady
Margaret Primary School; Little Sutton Primary School;
Parsloes Primary School.

Printed and bound in the UK

MIX
Paper | Supporting
responsible forestry
FSC **FSC™ C007454**
www.fsc.org

Acknowledgements
The publishers gratefully acknowledge the permission granted
to reproduce the copyright material in this book. Every effort
has been made to trace copyright holders and to obtain their
permission for the use of copyright material. The publishers
will gladly receive any information enabling them to rectify
any error or omission at the first opportunity.

p66t muratart/Shutterstock, p66b Gerdie Hutomo/
Shutterstock, p67t Hiroyuki Uchiyama/Getty Images,
p67c Elles Rijsdijk/Alamy Stock Photo, p67b & br IrinaK/
Shutterstock, p68 Caters News Agency Ltd/Shutterstock,
p69t Abeselom Zerit/Shutterstock, p69b Matthew Power/
Shutterstock.